American Photography 6

The annual of
American editorial,
advertising and poster,
book, promotion,
and unpublished
photography

American Photography 6

Edited by
Edward Booth-Clibborn
Design by Impress

Editor EDWARD BOOTH-CLIBBORN
Design IMPRESS
HANS TEENSMA JOAN LOCKHART AL CRANE
Project Director BONNIE CLAEYS
Associate Editor MARY YEUNG
Jacket and Dividing Page Photographs BRIAN SMALE

Special thanks to the School of Visual Arts for
providing the space and equipment for the
annual American Photography judging.

Captions and artwork in this book have been
supplied by the entrants. While every
effort has been made to ensure accuracy,
American Photography, Inc. does not under
any circumstances accept any responsibility for
errors or omissions.

If you are a practicing photographer or student
and would like to submit work
to the next annual competition, the deadline
this year is November 30.
For more information write to:

American Photography, Inc.
49 East 21st Street
New York, NY 10010
212-979-4500

Distributed in the United States and Canada by
Rizzoli International Publications
300 Park Avenue South
New York, NY 10010
ISBN 0-8478-5570-8

Distributed in the United Kingdom
and World Direct Mail:
Internos Books
18 Colville Road
London W3 8BL

Book trade for the rest of the world:
Hearst Books International
105 Madison Avenue
New York, NY 10016 USA

Printed and bound in Japan by Dai Nippon

American Photography 6

Contents

Introduction and Jury

Edward Booth-Clibborn

President

Five years on and still we're searching; looking for the finest photographs produced in the U.S. every year. It doesn't get any easier. The work gets better and our decisions get tougher. We get more submissions and our jury's hours get longer.

But nobody minds. In fact, we're glad it's this way. It means we can bring you the best of the best images each year.

And this year's no exception. The selection we've put together honors some established names, and some unknowns. Which is how it should be. For *American Photography* is a showcase for the best work being done, not a catalogue of the best-hyped names in town.

Fame will not buy a page in the book. Notoriety won't sway our jury. What matters is the work, and its quality. What may result from being included may be fame, or even notoriety. If that's the case, it's an accolade hard won. For we are determined to go on searching for the best, year after year.

And, as you'll see from these pages, we set very high standards.

GAEL TOWEY

Gael started her career at Studio Books, where she learned the history of photography "the hard way," pasting up books. She was promoted to Assistant Art Director when she designed two award-winning books. Gael combined her sense of history with her love of design and decoration when she became Art Director and later Creative Director at Clarkson N. Potter, where she worked on a series of highly successful style books. Since 1989, Gael has been Design Director of *HG* (House & Garden) Magazine. Her work has received several awards from AIGA, the Art Directors' Club, and The New York Book Show, among others.

MARILYN BABCOCK

Currently the Art Director at *L.A. Style* Magazine, Marilyn received both her BFA and MFA from the Otis Parsons Art Institute. She has been Designer at the Los Angeles Institute of Contemporary Art, working on the LAICA Journal. Marilyn has also served as Art Director at *California* Magazine, and more recently Associate Art Director at the L.A. Times Sunday Magazine.

HENRY CONNELL

Born in Cedar Falls, Iowa, Henry took his creative talents to Minnesota, studying at the Minneapolis College of Art and Design, and receiving his degree in filmmaking. Following graduation, he moved to New York City and has spent the past five years working as a designer and art director on various projects. Most recently Henry has served as Art Director at *Interview* Magazine.

DEREK UNGLESS

With formal training in illustration and graphic design, Derek has used his talents on various publications. Starting out as Designer at *Radio Times* in London, he went to Toronto where he was Associate Art Director at *Weekend* Magazine and also design consultant to *Esquire*. He later became Art Director at *Saturday Night* Magazine, Art Director at *Rolling Stone*, and eventually started his own firm, Angle Design Office. During this time, Derek served as Design Director at *HG*, redesigned the *Financial Times of Canada*, and designed the Readers' Catalog. More recently he was Art Director at *Vogue*, and is currently Creative Director at *Details*.

ELISABETH BIONDI

Born and educated in Germany, Elisabeth has been Director of Photography at *Vanity Fair* since 1985. Before joining *Vanity Fair*, she was Picture Editor at *Penthouse/Viva*, and worked on the start-up of *Omni* Magazine. Elisabeth has also served as Picture Editor at *American GEO* Magazine and *German GEO* in the United States. She has been named Picture Editor of the Year by the University of Missouri School of Photojournalism.

NEIL KRAFT

Neil started out as a "radical" photography student at the Rhode Island School of Design. Moving to New York after graduation, he became an assistant at Hurrah Productions, where he learned sound and film editing. He moved on to become a Producer at Epstein-Raboy, where he first worked on Barneys advertising. After a brief stint at Benton & Bowles, Neil joined Barneys in 1984 as Advertising Director, creating many of their trendsetting campaigns himself. This led to the birth of BNY Advertising, Barneys' in-house advertising department, which Neil has headed ever since.

Editorial

Albert Watson

Art Director FRED WOODWARD

Picture Editor LAURIE KRATOCHVIL

Writer DAVID FRICKE

Publication ROLLING STONE

Publisher STRAIGHT ARROW
PUBLISHERS, INC.

PORTRAITS OF MICK JAGGER
AND KEITH RICHARDS
FOR AN ARTICLE ENTITLED
"SATISFACTION?"
SEPTEMBER '89

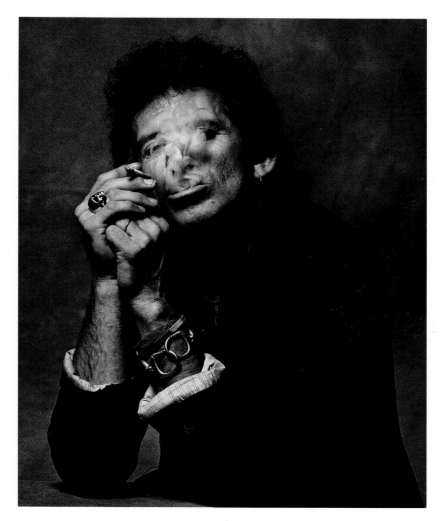

2

Albert Watson

Art Director FRED WOODWARD

Picture Editor LAURIE KRATOCHVIL

Writer ANTHONY DeCURTIS

Publication ROLLING STONE

Publisher STRAIGHT ARROW
PUBLISHERS, INC.

A CLOSE-UP OF KEITH RICHARDS
FOR A ROLLING STONE INTERVIEW,
OCTOBER '88

(Opposite)

Herb Ritts

Art Director MARILYN BABCOCK
Design Director MICHAEL BROCK
Picture Editor JODI NAKATSUKA
Publication L.A. STYLE
Publisher AMERICAN EXPRESS
PUBLICATIONS

FOR A FASHION FEATURE ENTITLED
"THINLY VEILED." APRIL '89

4

The Douglas Brothers

Art Director PAMELA BERRY
Picture Editor ALICE ALBERT
Publication SAVVY
Publisher FAMILY MEDIA
PUBLICATIONS

FOR AN ARTICLE ENTITLED
"YOU ARE ENOUGH"

(Opposite)

Geof Kern

Art Director LISA GABOR

Publication TAXI

Publisher FAMILY MEDIA INC.

THIS CHARMING COMPOSITION
IS FOR A FEATURE ENTITLED
"AFTER THE ROSE."

7

Geof Kern

Art Director FRED WOODWARD

Publication ROLLING STONE

Publisher STRAIGHT ARROW

PUBLISHERS, INC.

THIS GRAPHIC IMAGE
WAS USED IN THE FEATURE "THE 100
GREATEST ALBUMS OF THE '80'S."
APRIL '89

8-11

Geof Kern

Art Director RUTA FOX

Publication EXPOSURE MAGAZINE

GEOF KERN DEFINES
"POST MODERNISM" WITH A SERIES OF
ELEGANT, SURREALISTIC IMAGES.

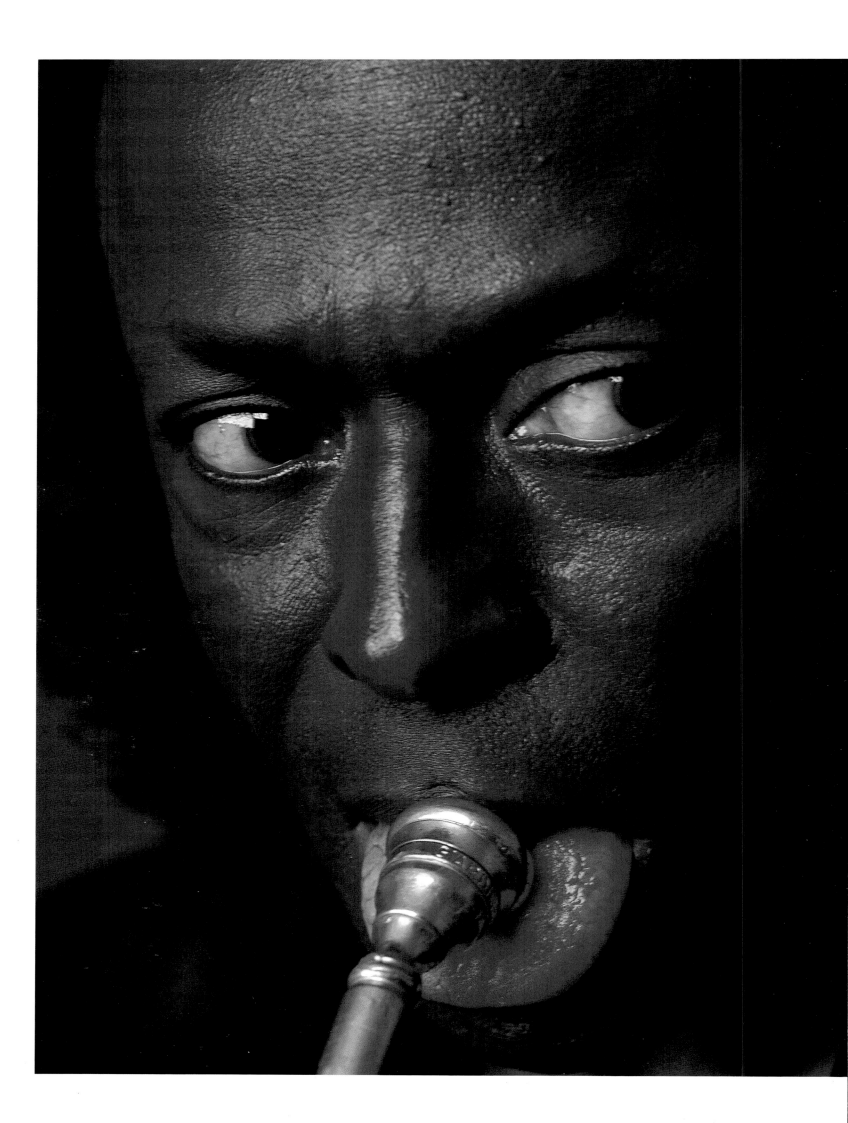

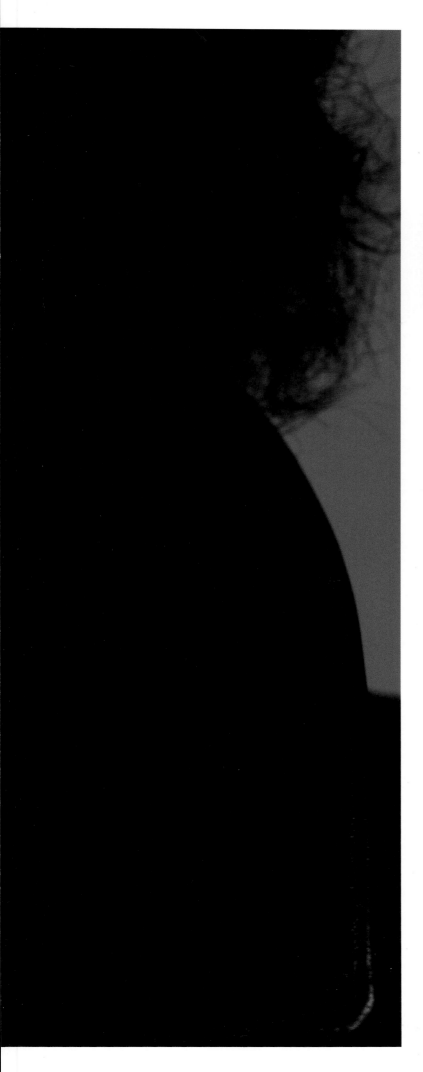

12-14

Annie Leibovitz

Art Director CHARLES CHURCHWARD

Picture Editor ELISABETH BIONDI

Writer JAMES KAPLAN

Publication VANITY FAIR

Publisher CONDÉ NAST PUBLICATIONS, INC.

THESE THREE IMAGES OF MILES DAVIS
ACCOMPANIED JAMES KAPLAN'S
PROFILE OF THE JAZZ MASTER.
AUGUST '89

15

Annie Leibovitz

Art Director CHARLES CHURCHWARD
Picture Editor ELISABETH BIONDI
Writer CHARLES MICHENER
Publication VANITY FAIR
Publisher CONDÉ NAST PUBLICATIONS, INC.

PORTRAIT OF AN EMOTIONAL
JESSYE NORMAN FOR A FEATURE ON
"DIVA FEVER," FEBRUARY '89

16-21
(Following three spreads)

Albert Watson

Art Director FRED WOODWARD
Picture Editor LAURIE KRATOCHVIL
Publication ROLLING STONE
Publisher STRAIGHT ARROW

PUBLISHERS, INC.

A SERIES OF SIX PORTRAITS WAS
PHOTOGRAPHED FOR A SPECIAL
FEATURE ENTITLED "LIVING LEGENDS."
SEPTEMBER '89

16

B.B. KING

17

JOHN LEE HOOKER

JUNIOR WELLS

BUDDY GUY

20

BO DIDDLEY

21

ALBERT KING

22
(Left)

Annie Leibovitz

Art Director CHARLES CHURCHWARD
Picture Editor ELISABETH BIONDI
Writer LESLIE BENNETTS
Publication VANITY FAIR
Publisher CONDÉ NAST PUBLICATIONS, INC.

AN INTIMATE PORTRAIT OF
STAR-CROSSED LOVERS MIKE TYSON
AND ROBIN GIVENS FOR "TYSON TURMOIL"
BY LESLIE BENNETTS, NOVEMBER '88

23

Timothy White

Art Director FRED WOODWARD
Picture Editor LAURIE KRATOCHVIL
Publication ROLLING STONE
Publisher STRAIGHT ARROW
PUBLISHERS, INC.

PORTRAIT OF FEISTY COMEDIENNE
SANDRA BERNHARD, FOR
"WHO'S AFRAID OF SANDRA BERNHARD?"
NOVEMBER '88

24

Max Aguilera-Hellweg

Art Director   NANCY DUCKWORTH
Picture Editor   ALYSON MORELEY
Writer   REX WEINER
Publication   LOS ANGELES TIMES
MAGAZINE
Publisher   LOS ANGELES TIMES

THREE IMAGES FROM REX WEINER'S
ARTICLE, "LA BOYLÉ," JUNE '89

PORTRAIT OF CECILIA BLANCO

25

MARIACHIS IN THEIR TRADITIONAL
"HORSEMAN'S SUIT"

PORTRAIT OF EL COCHERO,
A FOUNDER OF LA BOYLÉ

28

Brian Smale

Art Director STEVE HOFFMAN

Picture Editor BOB MITCHELL

Publication SPORTS ILLUSTRATED

Publisher TIME WARNER

FIVE PORTRAITS OF NFL PLAYERS
WERE FEATURED IN THE ARTICLE,
"SOARING INTO THE 90'S"
SEPTEMBER '89

NFL PLAYER TIM HARRIS

27
(Left)

NFL PLAYER MICHAEL IRVIN

NFL PLAYERS BRIAN AND BENNIE BLADES

NFL PLAYER TOM NEWBERRY

31

NFL PLAYER BUBBY BRISTER

Richard Avedon

Art Director ROBERT PRIEST

Writer DAVID BRESKIN

Publication G Q

Publisher CONDÉ NAST PUBLICATIONS, INC.

A DIFFERENT KIND OF SHOOTING STAR,
MICHAEL JORDON, FOR THE ARTICLE,
"MICHAEL JORDON IN HIS OWN ORBIT"
MARCH 1989

Abbas

Art Director CHARLES CHURCHWARD

Picture Editor ELISABETH BIONDI

Writer T.D. ALLMAN

Publication VANITY FAIR

Publisher CONDÉ NAST PUBLICATIONS

TWO IMAGES FROM THE ARTICLE,
"ON THE ROAD WITH ARAFAT,"
FEBRUARY '89

SHOWN ABOVE YASSIR ARAFAT AS HE
IS LEAVING THE RESIDENCE OF THE P.L.O.
REPRESENTATIVE IN LA MARSA, NEAR TUNIS

34

YASSIR ARAFAT IN A RARE
RELAXING MOMENT

(Opposite)

Geof Kern

Art Director JOHN KORPICS

Publication REGARDIE'S

Writer MARK PERRY

Publisher REGARDIE'S MAGAZINE, INC.

THIS HAUNTING PORTRAIT RECREATES
AMERICAN SPY WILLIAM BUCKLEY'S
LAST DAYS OF CAPTIVITY FOR THE
FEBRUARY '89 COVER.

35

Robert Whitman

Art Director OLIVIER VAN DOORNE

Picture Editor LINDA MORREN

Writer JOHN MOTAVALLI

Publication MAX

Publisher SOPREFI

A BOXER IN THE MIRROR,
IS FEATURED IN "MAX," A FRENCH
MAGAZINE, FOR A PIECE ON
BOXERS IN NEW YORK,
JUNE '89

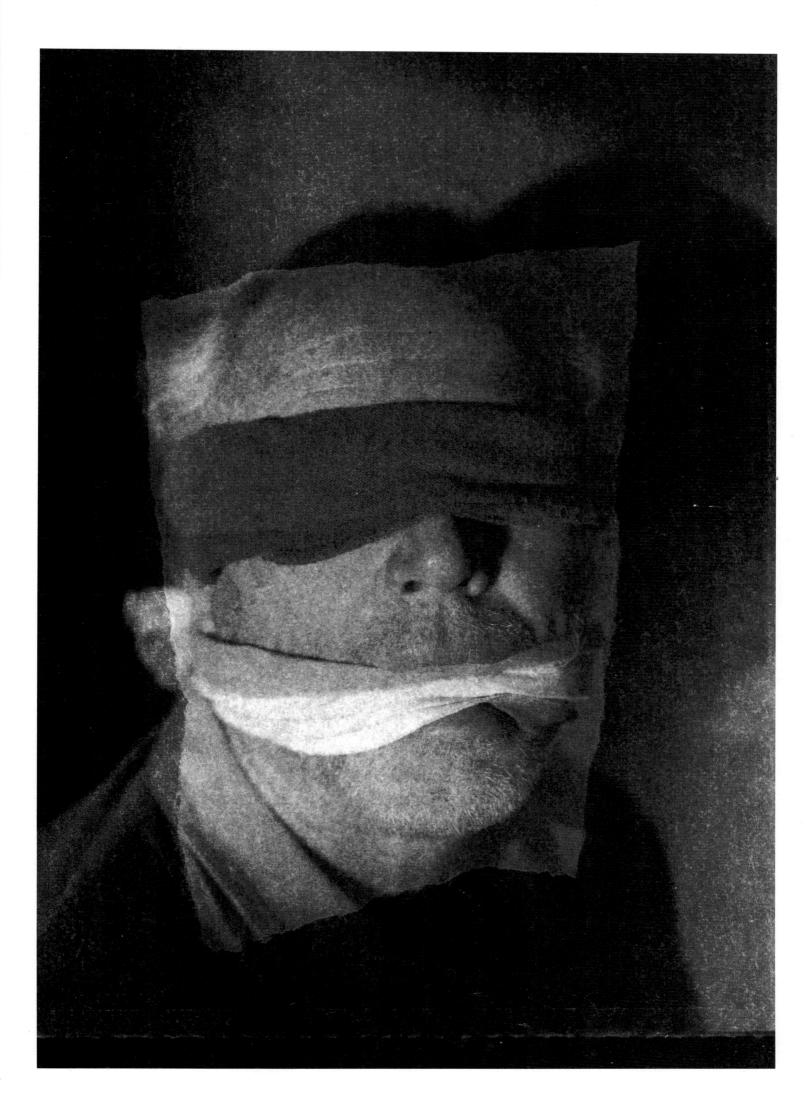

37-39

Mary Ellen Mark

Picture Editor COLIN JACOBSON

Writer PETER DUNN

Publication THE INDEPENDENT MAGAZINE

THE SENIOR OLYMPICS, AN EVENT
HIGHLIGHTED IN "THE SPIRIT OF
ST. LOUIS," AUGUST 1989

Picture Editor CATHY RYAN

Publication THE NEW YORK TIMES

THE SENIOR OLYMPICS WERE ALSO
FEATURED IN A NEW YORK TIMES
MAGAZINE PIECE, "VICTORIES OF
THE SPIRIT," AUGUST 1989.

40

Charles Shotwell

Art Director LAWRENCE WOODHULL

Picture Editor SARA ELDER

Designer MICHAEL MILLER

Design Director BETT MCLEAN

Writer JEFF MATTESON

Publication VETERINARY PRACTICE
MANAGEMENT

Publisher WHITTLE COMMUNICATIONS

THIS PAMPERED POODLE WAS
FEATURED IN THE ARTICLE,
"PET PAMPERING, AMERICAN STYLE."
WINTER '88-'89

42
(Right)

Mark Seliger

Art Director FRED WOODWARD
Picture Editor JIM FRANCO
Publication ROLLING STONE
Publisher STRAIGHT ARROW
PUBLISHERS, INC.

THESE MEMORABLE EXPRESSIONS
WERE TAKEN AT THE COMEDY
CONVENTION, FOR THE FEATURE,
"100 CHARACTERS IN SEARCH."

41

Christopher Little

Art Director COURTNEY BROWN
Picture Editor M.C. MARDEN
Publication PEOPLE WEEKLY
Publisher TIME WARNER

A HUMOROUS PORTRAIT OF
NBC'S FUNNY MAN WILLARD SCOTT,
FOR THE ARTICLE, "WILLARD SCOTT
IS BLOWING HIS TOP," MARCH '89.

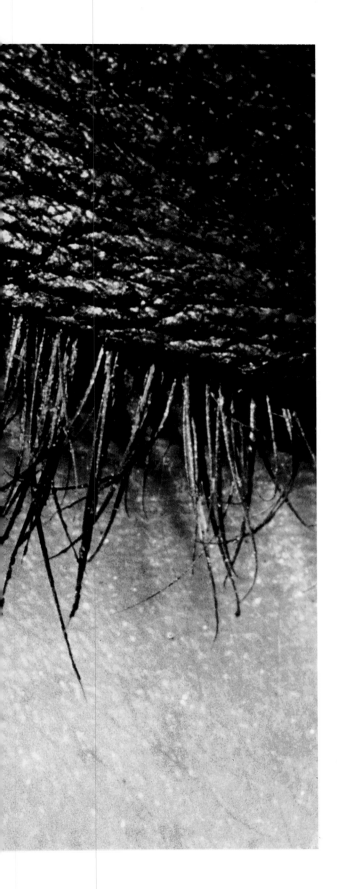

43-47

Gabriella Imperatori

Art Director GABRIELLA IMPERATORI

Writer GEORGES BATAILLE

Publication N.Y. WRITER

Publisher AMERICAN EXPOSITIONS

THESE FIVE SURREALISTIC, EXTREME
CLOSE-UPS WERE USED IN A SPECIAL
FEATURE, "THE STORY OF THE EYE."
SPRING '89

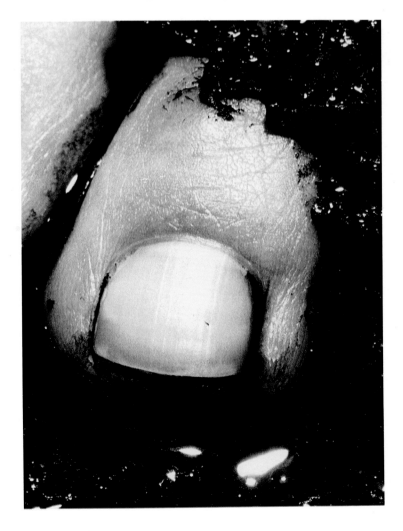

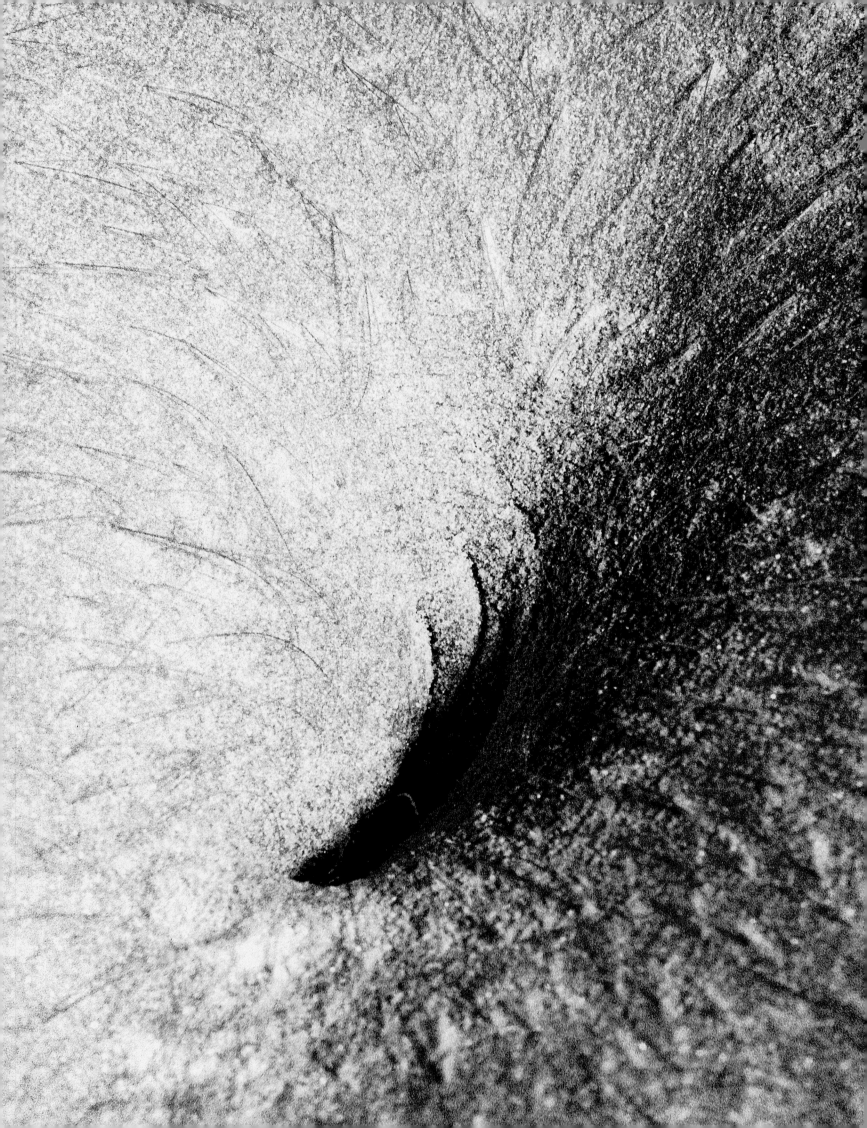

Lisa Powers

Art Director CHRIS LEONE
Publication ART & ANTIQUES
Publisher ALLISON PUBLICATIONS, INC.

TWO PHOTOGRAPHS REALISTICALLY
RECREATING THE WARMTH OF
KITCHENS FROM THE PAST,
FOR THE ARTICLE, "40'S KITCHENS"

Rocky Schenck

Art Director DOUG RENFRO
Writer LEA ANN LEMING
Publication SPECIAL REPORT
Publisher WHITTLE COMMUNICATIONS

GLAMOROUS PORTRAITS OF
FIVE SUPERSTAR IMPERSONATORS
HIGHLIGHTED IN THE ARTICLE
"GREAT PRETENDERS"

RANDY ALLEN AS JUDY GARLAND

MR. JIMMY JAMES AS MARILYN MONROE

52

ELGIN KENNA AS CHER

53

SHAWN MICHAELS AS DIANA ROSS

54

CHARLES PIERCE AS BETTE DAVIS

55

Tony Costa

Art Director COURTNEY BROWN
Publication PEOPLE WEEKLY
Publisher TIME WARNER

BETTE DAVIS WITH
HER FAVORITE PROP

56-60

Albert Watson

Art Director MARILYN BABCOCK
Picture Editor JODI NAKATSUKA
Publication L.A. STYLE
Publisher AMERICAN EXPRESS
PUBLICATIONS

FIVE PHOTOS FOR THE FASHION
LAYOUT, "BLACK TIE EVENTS"

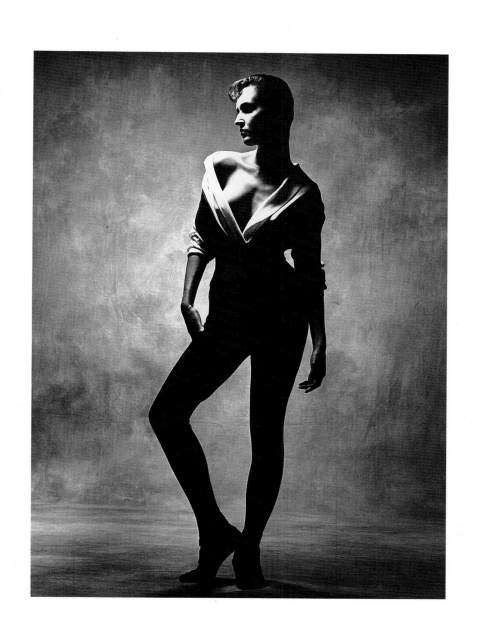

(Opposite)

Guzman

Art Director MARILYN BABCOCK

Picture Editor JODI NAKATSUKA

Publication L.A. STYLE

Publisher AMERICAN EXPRESS

PUBLICATIONS

FOR THE "COAT COUTURE"
FASHION SPREAD

(Opposite)

Herb Ritts

Art Director MARILYN BABCOCK
Design Director MICHAEL BROCK
Picture Editor JODI NAKATSUKA
Publication L.A. STYLE
Publisher AMERICAN EXPRESS
PUBLICATIONS

THE JULY '89 COVER

63

Sheila Metzner

Art Director MARY SHANAHAN
Publication FRENCH VOGUE
Publisher CONDÉ NAST PUBLICATIONS, INC.

THIS IMAGE OF A MODERN BRACELET
WAS CREATED FOR A FASHION
LAYOUT ENTITLED "MAN RAY."
APRIL '89

65
(Right)

Herb Ritts

Art Director CHARLES CHURCHWARD

Picture Editor ELISABETH BIONDI

Writer PAUL ROSENFIELD

Publication VANITY FAIR

Publisher CONDÉ NAST PUBLICATIONS, INC.

KIM BASINGER STRIKES A REVEALING
POSE FOR THE FEATURE,
"KIM—IN THE SWIM," JUNE 1989.

64

Herb Ritts

Art Director MARILYN BABCOCK

Design Director MICHAEL BROCK

Picture Editor JODI NAKATSUKA

Publication L.A. STYLE

Publisher AMERICAN EXPRESS

PUBLICATIONS

THE SEPTEMBER '89 COVER

Stuart Watson

Art Director MARILYN BABCOCK
Picture Editor JODI NAKATSUKA
Publication L.A. STYLE
Publisher AMERICAN EXPRESS
PUBLICATIONS

AN ELEGANT IMAGE OF
A WOMAN WITH PEARLS FOR
THE FASHION LAYOUT,
"FINAL TOUCHES"

67

Josef Astor

Art Director CHARLES CHURCHWARD
Picture Editor ELISABETH BIONDI
Publication VANITY FAIR
Publisher CONDÉ NAST PUBLICATIONS, INC.

PORTRAIT OF LEGGY UMA THURMAN
WAS FEATURED IN
VANITY FAIR'S "SPOTLIGHT"

Phillip Dixon

Art Director   MARILYN BABCOCK
Picture Editor   JODI NAKATSUKA
Publication   L.A. STYLE
Publisher   AMERICAN EXPRESS
PUBLICATIONS

FOR THE FASHION LAYOUT
"IT'S A WRAP"

68

Mark Mainguy

Art Director   SUSAN CASEY
Writer   JULIE OVENELL-CARTER
Publication   WEST MAGAZINE
Publisher   THE GLOBE AND MAIL

"SHADOWLAND GHOST STORIES"
FEATURED THIS EERIE PORTRAIT
OF A YOUNG WOMAN.
SEPTEMBER '89

Nick Knight

Art Director CHARLES CHURCHWARD
Picture Editor ELIZABETH BIONDI
Writer CHRISTA WORTHINGTON
Publication VANITY FAIR
Publisher CONDÉ NAST PUBLICATIONS, INC.

A SENSUOUS SHOT OF
NEW SCREEN SIREN BRIDGET FONDA
FOR "GROWING FONDA,"
NOVEMBER '88

Brian Smale

Designer KATHI ROTA
Picture Editor LAURIE KRATOCHVIL
Writer CARL BERNSTEIN
Publication ROLLING STONE
Publisher STRAIGHT ARROW
PUBLISHERS, INC.

PORTRAIT OF CARL BERNSTEIN
FOR AN ARTICLE HE WROTE
ENTITLED "LOYALITIES"

72

C h r i s   S a n d e r s

Art Director CLAUDIA LEBENTHAL

Publication 7 DAYS MAGAZINE

FOR A FEATURE ENTITLED
"THE GEOGRAPHY OF FASHION,"
PHOTO WAS TAKEN AT
BAROCCO RESTAURANT

73-75

Josef Astor

Art Director DEBBIE SMITH

Picture Editor GREG POND

Publication TAXI

Publisher FAMILY MEDIA INC.

THREE STYLISH, SURREALISTIC IMAGES
FOR A FASHION LAYOUT ENTITLED
"SUSPENDED ANIMATION,"
NOVEMBER 1989

76

Mick Hales

Art Director DEREK UNGLESS

Picture Editor SUSAN GOLDBERGER

Writer ALAN EMMET

Publications HOUSE & GARDEN

Publisher CONDÉ NAST PUBLICATIONS, INC.

NATIVE WHITE PINES ON A STEEP
BLUFF OVERLOOKING LAKE WABAN,
MASSACHUSETTS; TAKEN AT
HUNNEWELL GARDEN FOR AN ARTICLE
ENTITLED "FAMILY TREES"

Geof Kern

Art Director B.W. HONEYCUTT

Writer HENRY "DUTCH" HOLLAND

Publication SPY

Publisher SPY PUBLISHING PARTNERS

THIS POETIC ABSTRACTION
APPEARED IN SPY'S REVIEW
OF REVIEWERS COLUMN,
FOR "THE STORY OF THEIR LIVES."
AUGUST '89

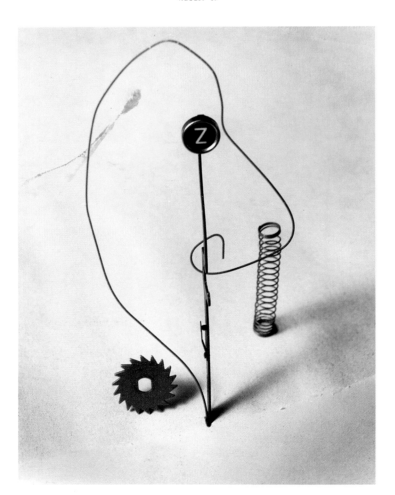

D e b o r a h   S a m u e l

Art Director CARMEN DUNJKO

Writer IVOR SHAPIRO

Publication SATURDAY NIGHT MAGAZINE

Publisher HOLLINGER, INC.

FOR AN ARTICLE ENTITLED
"FINDING WORDS"

79-82

N e a l   S l a v i n

Picture Editor KATHLEEN KLECH
Writer SIMON WINCHESTER
Publication CONDÉ NAST TRAVELER
Publisher CONDÉ NAST PUBLICATIONS, INC.

FOUR TIMELESS IMAGES TAKEN AT
THE ROYAL GEOGRAPHIC SOCIETY
FOR "THE HIGH PRIESTS OF WANDERLUST,"
AN ARTICLE BY SIMON WINCHESTER,
JANUARY '90

POPULAR
POPULAR SCIENCE
SCIENCE
FOUNDED MONTHLY 1872

A SHADY TRICK

Hat Frames -- Ta...
Elastics -- Marquisettes...
Wires...
36 West 36th Street, New Yo...
CHickering 4-0642-...
36

DRINK
Coca-...
"How about a Coke"

...and Refreshing

J e r e m y   S h a t a n

Art Director R O B E R T   P R I E S T

Writer T H O M A S   H I N E

Designer C H A R L E N E   B E N S O N

Publication G Q

Publisher C O N D É   N A S T   P U B L I C A T I O N S   I N C .

AN IMAGE FROM THE FLEA MARKET
ACCOMPANIED THOMAS HINE'S ARTICLE,
"THE JOY OF KITSCH."
OCTOBER '89

84-94

Kurt Markus

Art Director RIP GEORGES

Picture Editor TEMPLE SMITH

Writer LEE EISENBERG

Publication ESQUIRE

Publisher HEARST CORPORATION

ELEVEN POETIC IMAGES OF AMERICA'S
FAVORITE PASTIME FOR "THE GAME
WITHOUT VIOLINS OR APOLOGIES,"
APRIL 1989

95-97

Lee Crum

Art Director RIP GEORGES

Picture Editor TEMPLE SMITH

Writer JOHN ED BRADLEY

Publication ESQUIRE

Publisher HEARST CORPORATION

THE PLAYFUL CHARM OF
DENNIS QUAID AS JERRY LEE LEWIS
FOR THE ARTICLE,
"GOODNESS GRACIOUS,"
MARCH '89

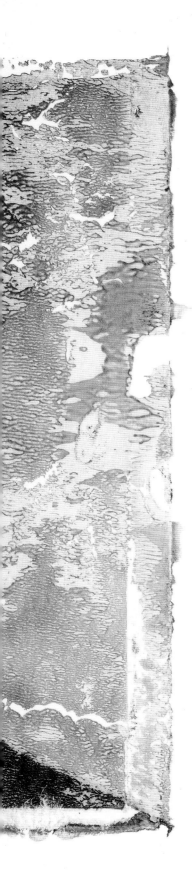

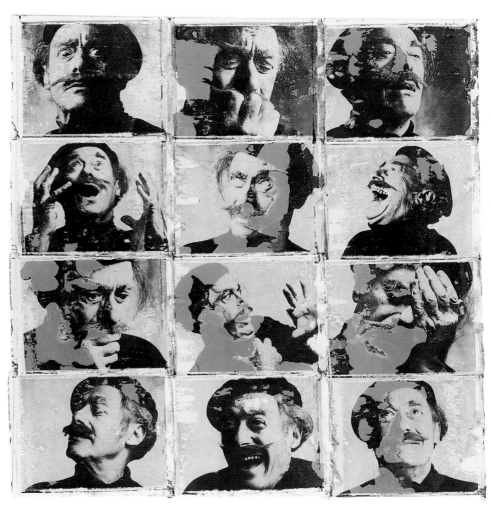

100
(Following spread)

Taro Yamasaki

Art Director COURTNEY BROWN

Picture Editor M.C. MARDEN

Publication PEOPLE WEEKLY

Publisher TIME WARNER

A PHOTO DOCUMENTING EFFORTS
TO SAVE TRAPPED WHALES IN ALASKA,
NOVEMBER '88

98-99

Michael Regnier

Art Director STEVE KEETLE

Writer GLORIA HOCHMAN

Publication STAR MAGAZINE

Publisher THE KANSAS CITY

STAR COMPANY

THESE MULTIPLE IMAGES DEPICT
THE PAIN AND TRAGEDY OF
MANIC DEPRESSION, FOR THE ARTICLE,
"A CURSE OF GENIUS." OCTOBER '89

101

Chip Simons

Art Director MARY WORKMAN

Publication TENNESSEE ILLUSTRATED

Publisher WHITTLE COMMUNICATIONS

FOR A FEATURE ENTITLED
"BACK TO TENNESSEE"

RALLY, JACKSON

102

LOOKOUT MOUNTAIN, CHATTANOOGA

103

FIREHOUSE LEWISBURG

104

PUMPKIN PATCH,
CUMBERLAND PLATEAU

105

MISSISSIPPI RIVER, MEMPHIS

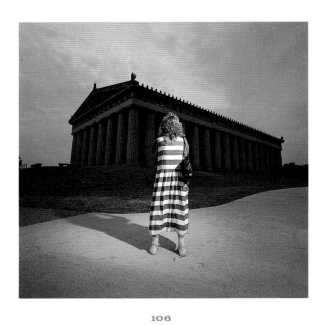

106

THE PARTHENON, NASHVILLE

107

ROUTE 64, LAWRENCEBURG

108

TENNESSEE RIVER, DECATUR

109

GRACELAND, MEMPHIS

110

ROUTE 125, MONTEZUMA

Advertising and Posters

111

Timothy Greenfield-Sanders

Art Director DOUGLAS LLOYD
Client BNY ADVERTISING

PORTRAITS OF THREE ACTORS IN
ADVERTISEMENTS FOR BARNEY'S, NEW YORK

ABOVE, JULIAN SANDS
PUBLISHED IN NEW YORK MAGAZINE

DEAN STOCKWELL

113

ROBERT TOWNSEND, PUBLISHED IN GQ

114-116

Marc Hauser

Agency LISKA DESIGN

Client BRADLEY PRINTING

THESE THREE IMAGES WERE USED
TO DEMONSTRATE THE QUALITY
OF BRADLEY PRINTING.

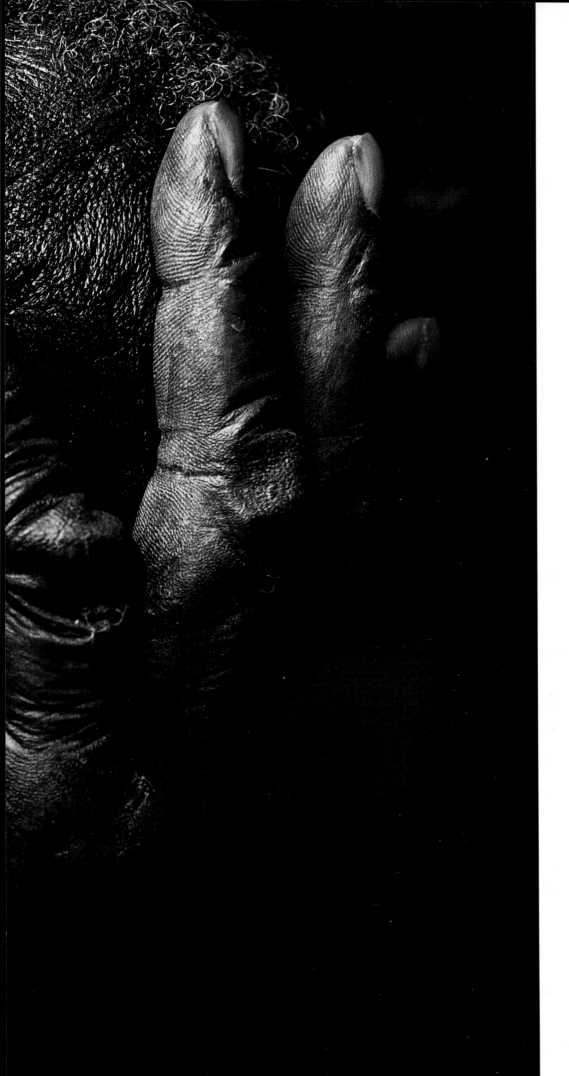

117

Gregory Heisler

Art Director STEPHEN HALL

Agency RUMRILL-HOYT, INC.

Client EASTMAN KODAK

THIS PORTRAIT OF LUIS SARRIA,
FORMER MASSEUR TO MUHAMMAD ALI,
WAS FEATURED IN KODAK'S AD CAMPAIGN,
"THE LANGUAGE OF BLACK-AND-WHITE."

118

C.B. Harding

Art Director PIERRE OUELETTE

A STARK IMAGE OF A COMPUTER CHIP
APPEARED IN AN AD IN
ELECTRONIC ENGINEERING TIMES.

119

Nick Vedros

Art Director JOHN MULLER

Agency MULLER & CO.

Client KANSAS CITY ART

DIRECTORS CLUB

THIS HANDSOME FACE WAS
SHOWCASED IN THE KANSAS CITY
ART DIRECTORS CLUB'S
CALL FOR ENTRIES ANNOUNCEMENT.

Geof Kern

Art Director FRED WOODWARD

Client AIGA

AN ELEGANT IMAGE FOR
AN AIGA PROMOTIONAL POSTER

Books

121-125

Timothy Hursley

Book AMERICAN CLASSICIST

Writer ELIZABETH DOWLING

Client ATLANTA HISTORICAL SOCIETY

THESE FIVE IMAGES HIGHLIGHT THE DESIGNS
OF ARCHITECT PHILIP TRAMMELL SHUTZE.

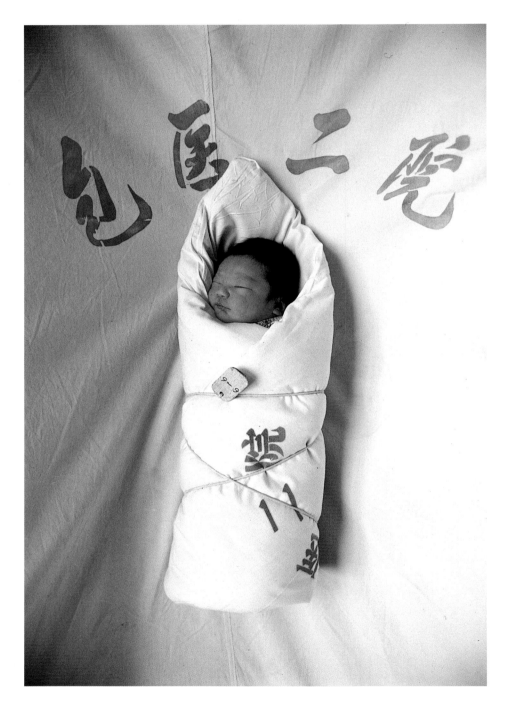

126

Nick Kelsh

Book A DAY IN THE LIFE OF CHINA
Publisher COLLINS PUBLISHERS

THIS AND THE FOLLOWING FOUR
PHOTOS ARE A SAMPLING FROM A BOOK
PROJECT INVOLVING 100 PHOTOGRAPHERS
ON THE EVENTS OF APRIL 15, 1989.

THE COVER PHOTO OF A BABY BUNDLE
WAS SHOT IN THE BAOTOU REGION
OF INNER MONGOLIA.

127

B r u n o   B a r b e y

UIGHUR WOMEN IN THE REMOTE
MOSLEM CITY OF KASHGAR

Jay Dickman

KAZAKH HORSEMEN

129

Dilip Mehta

BUDDHIST MONKS AT THE LABRANG TIBETAN
MONASTERY IN GANSU

130

Paul Chesley

A COUPLE WAITING FOR THE TRAIN
AT THE BEIJING STATION

131

Herman LeRoy Emmet

Book FRUIT TRAMPS

Publisher UNIVERSITY OF

NEW MEXICO PRESS

HERMAN LEROY EMMET SPENT NINE YEARS
DOCUMENTING THE ISOLATED LIVES OF
A FAMILY OF MIGRANT FARM WORKERS,
THE TINDALS. THE BOOK RECEIVED A
PULITZER PRIZE NOMINATION.

OLCOTT, NEW YORK, 1984

132

LOXAHATCHEE, FLORIDA, 1981

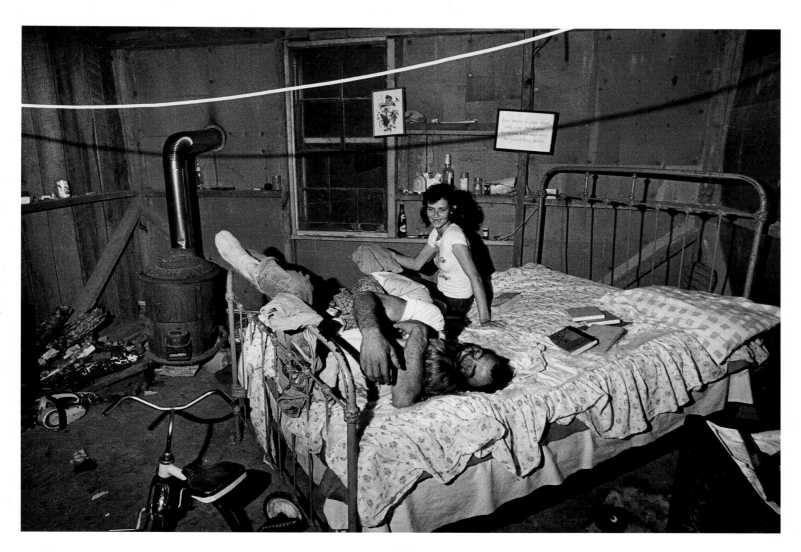

133

EDNEYVILLE, NORTH CAROLINA, 1979

134

SALUDA, SOUTH CAROLINA, 1979

135

FT. PIERCE, FLORIDA, 1986

Promotion

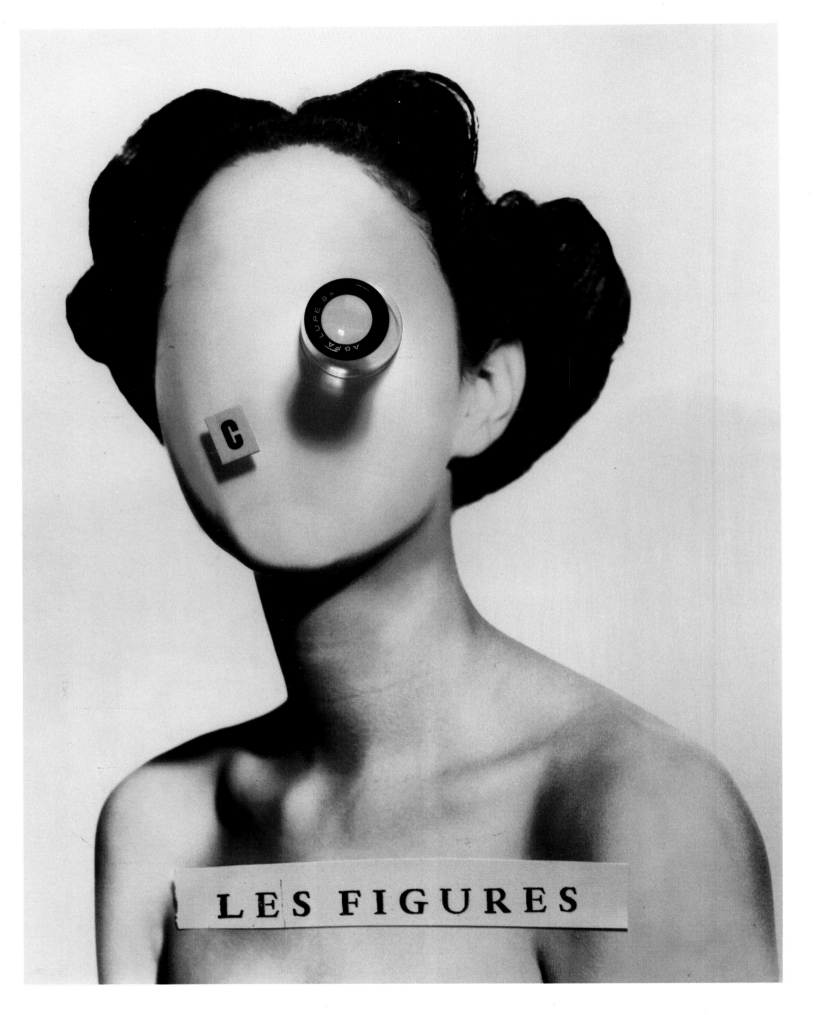

G e o f   K e r n

Client CONCRETE DESIGN

Art Director JILLY SIMONS

A FACELESS BEAUTY WAS
USED IN A PROMOTIONAL BROCHURE
FOR CHICAGO'S CONCRETE DESIGN.

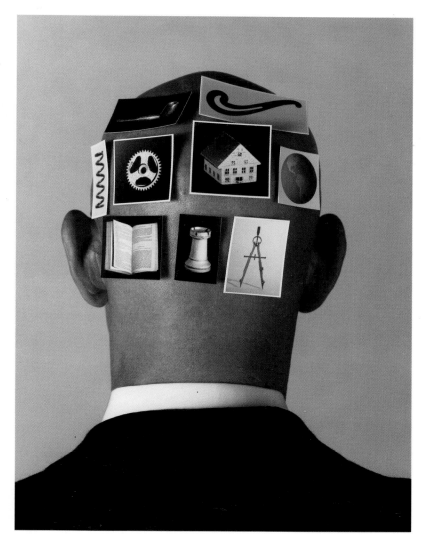

137

G e o f   K e r n

Art Director B.W. HONEYCUTT

Client SPY PUBLISHING PARTNERS

THIS THOUGHT-PROVOKING PHOTO
WAS SHOWCASED IN A
SELF-PROMOTIONAL BROCHURE
FOR SPY MAGAZINE.

Brian Smale

Client ROLLING STONE

THE COLOR VERSION OF THIS PHOTO
OF MICHAEL STIPE WAS PUBLISHED IN
ROLLING STONE. THE BLACK-AND-WHITE
VERSION WAS USED AS A
SELF-PROMOTIONAL MAILER.

(Right)

Timothy White

Client A & M RECORDS

PUBLICITY PHOTO FOR
SINGER JOE JACKSON

140-141

Walter Urie

Art Director MARGARET YASUDA

Agency DOUGLAS BOYD DESIGN

Client SCOTT NEWMAN CENTER

THESE TWO SOBERING IMAGES
WERE SHOT FOR A BROCHURE ON
SUBSTANCE ABUSE PREVENTION.

Gabriella Imperatori

SPARSE AND GRAPHIC,
THESE STILL LIFES WERE USED FOR
GABRIELLA IMPERATORI'S
SELF-PROMOTIONAL MAILERS.

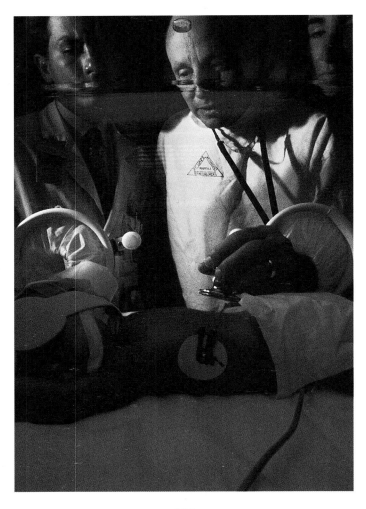

144

Jim Sims

Client BAYLOR COLLEGE OF MEDICINE

THIS PORTRAIT OF A CARING DOCTOR
WAS USED IN A FUND-RAISING BROCHURE
FOR BAYLOR COLLEGE OF MEDICINE.
NOVEMBER '88

145-150

Kurt Markus

Agency STUDIO SUPERCOMPASS,
TOKYO, JAPAN

SIX PHOTOGRAPHS FROM A CATALOG
ENTITLED "Y'S FOR LIVING"
FEBRUARY '89

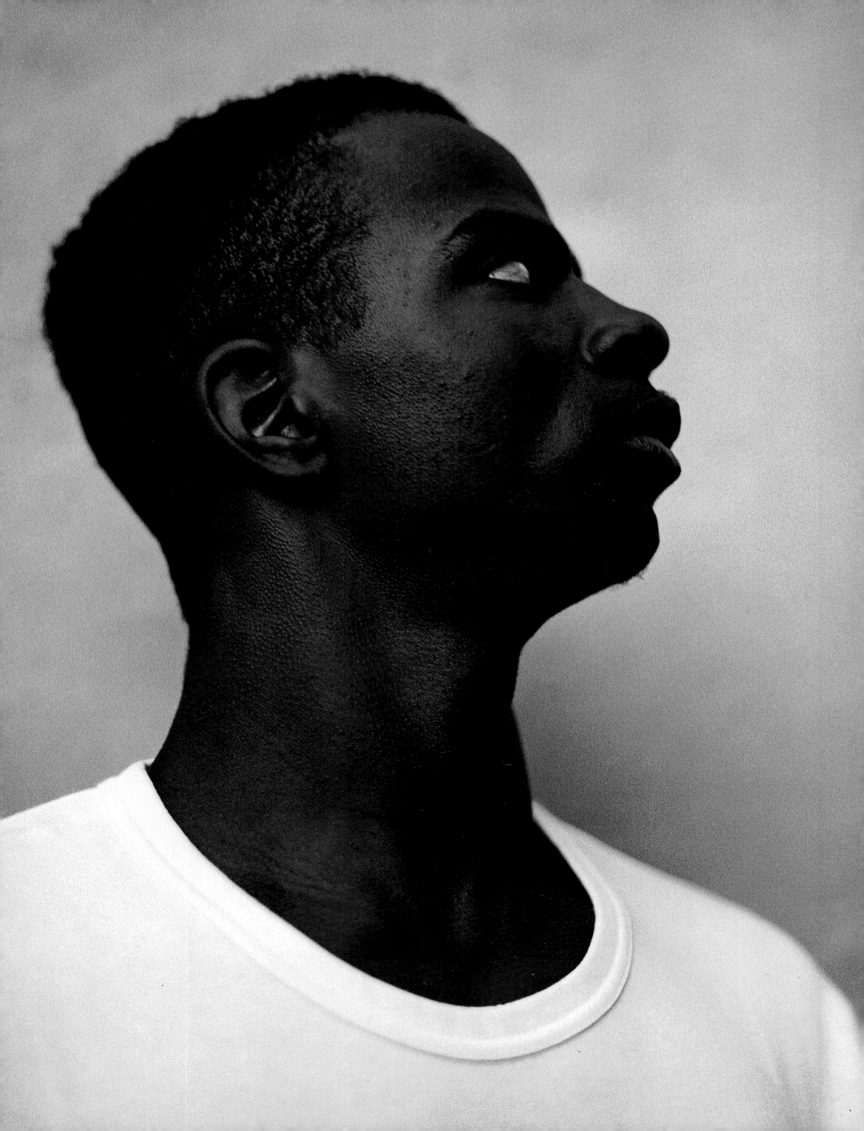

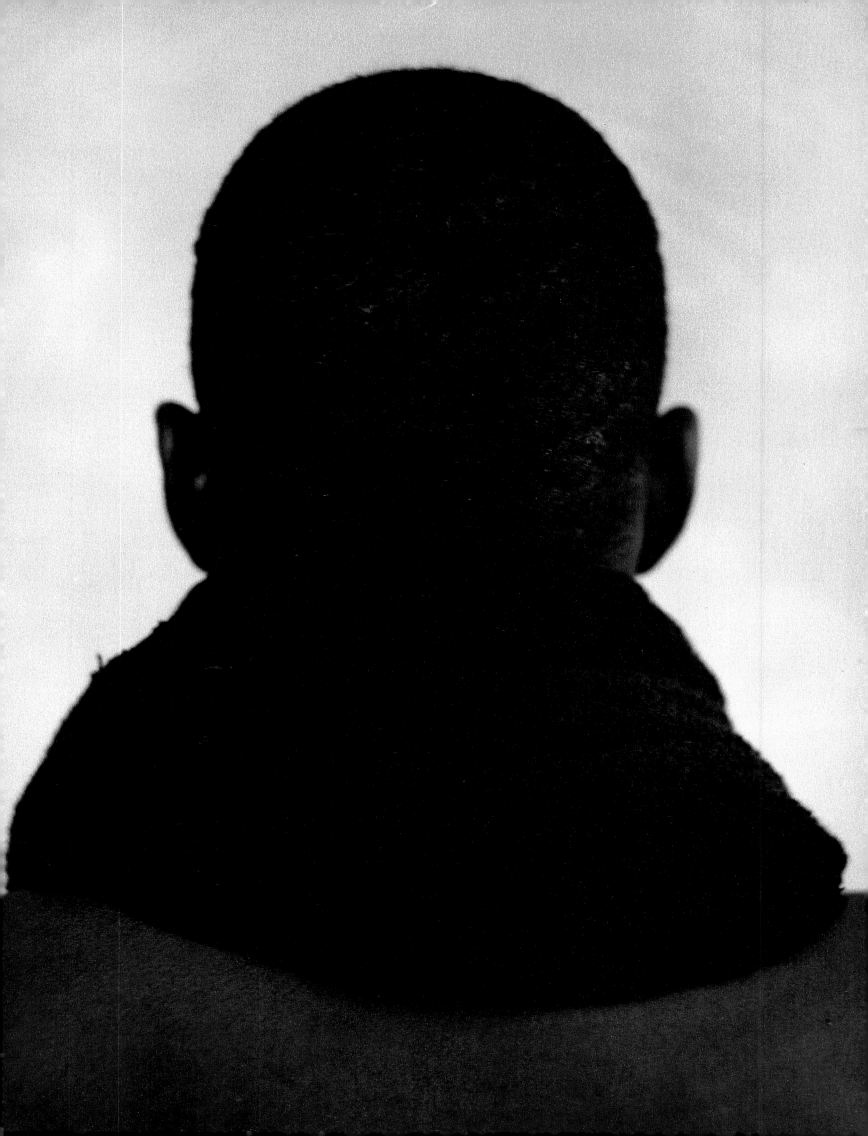

Unpublished Work

152

Daniel Winters

TWO SELF-ASSIGNED PROJECTS

SHOWN HERE, A MAN IN WATER

151
(Previous spread)

William Volckening

THIS IMAGE OF A LINE OF
CLEAN LAUNDRY TAKES ON
A SPIRITUAL OVERTONE.

153

SCULPTOR JOHN WELLS IN HIS
CONCRETE TV

154
(Left)

Craig Cutler

FROM A PERSONAL SERIES ENTITLED
"GEOMETRIC SOUTHWEST"

155-156

Christopher Boas

TWO PERSONAL PIECES EXAMINING
A MODERN DILEMMA,
"LIVING WITH MEGALITHS."

Daniel Borris

THIS PERSONAL PIECE IS ENTITLED
"CORY AT 11."

158-160

John Dyer

THREE PORTRAITS OF BOXERS
IN SAN ANTONIO, TEXAS FROM THE
PHOTOGRAPHER'S PORTFOLIO

161

Eleni Mylonas

TWO SELF-ASSIGNED IMAGES.

A SMASHED VEHICLE BECOMES
"UNIVERSAL SALVAGE V"

162
"EARTH TO EARTH"

163-164

Jim Sims

TWO IMAGES TAKEN IN EL SALVADOR,
WHEN JIM SIMS WAS PARTICIPATING
IN THE NORTH AMERICAN WITNESS
FOR PEACE AND REPOPULATION MISSION.

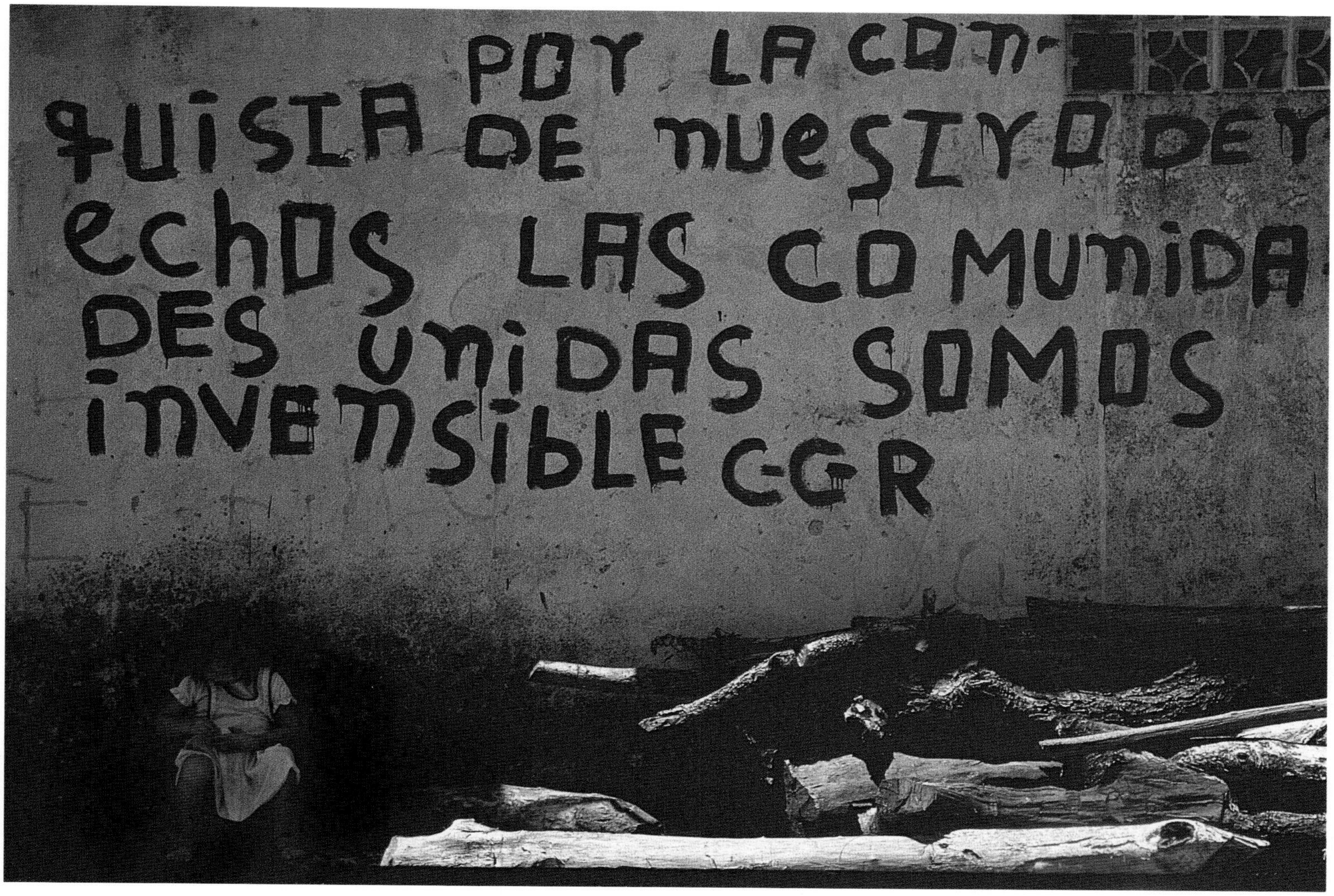
POR LA CON-
QUISTA DE NUESTRO DER
ECHOS LAS COMUNIDA
DES UNIDAS SOMOS
INVENSIBLE C-GR

165-166

E t h e l   W o l v o v i t z

ITALIAN AMERICANS CELEBRATING
THE ST. GIGLIO FESTIVAL
IN WILLIAMSBURG, BROOKLYN

167

D a n i e l   P r o c t o r

A POLAROID TRANSFER OF
A MAN'S PROFILE

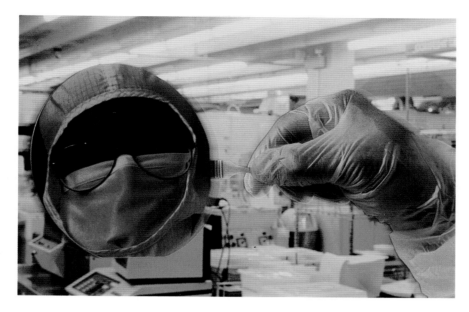

168

Jon A. Rembold

Client INSIGHT MAGAZINE

AN OUTTAKE FROM A SHOOT ON AT&T

169
(Following spread)

George Steinmetz

Client LIFE MAGAZINE

A DOLPHIN LANGUAGE TRAINING
SESSION WAS COMMISSIONED FOR
A FEATURE ON DOLPHIN MANIA.

170-171

S k i p   D e a n

TWO PERSONAL STILL LIVES

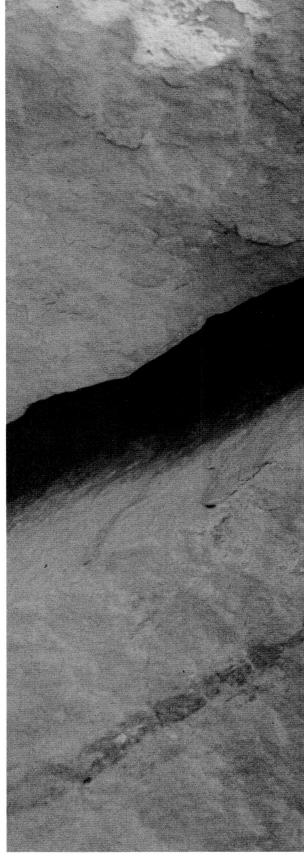

172-173

Sheila Metzner

Client CONDÉ NAST PUBLICATIONS, INC.

FOUR CORNERS OF THE SOUTHWEST SHOT
FOR CONDÉ NAST TRAVELER MAGAZINE

TOP, THE BRIDGE MARTIAN,
ARCHES NATIONAL PARK, UTAH

BOTTOM, MESA VERDE, COLORADO

POINT OF IMPACT,
CHACO CANYON, ARIZONA

S h e i l a   M e t z n e r

Client   C O N D É   N A S T   P U B L I C A T I O N S ,   I N C .

THIS PIECE WAS COMMISSIONED
BY ITALIAN VOGUE FOR THE
ASSIGNMENT "METAL OBJECTS."

175

S i l a s   J a c k s o n

THREE MEN AT A PARTY ENTITLED
"DIETER'S BIRTHDAY"

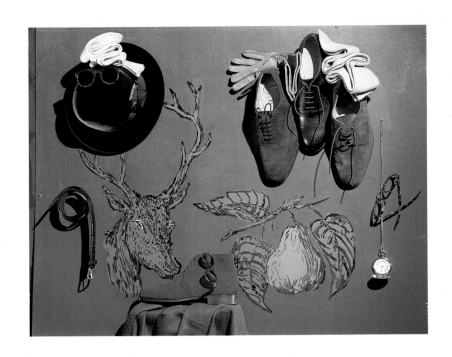

177-179

James Wojcik

Art Director ROBERT PRIEST

Client CONDÉ NAST PUBLICATIONS, INC.

FASHION STILL LIFES
COMMISSIONED BY GQ

180

Charlie Pizzarello

"HOMAGE TO GRACE"
IS ONE IN A SERIES COMMISSIONED
BY HAT DESIGNER PARRISH.

181

Mark Hanauer

MARK HANAUER GIVES LEGS
YET ANOTHER FRESH ANGLE.

Photographs by Artists

182

Sandra Tasca

AN AMBITIOUS PORTRAIT EXPERIMENT
EXECUTED WITH BLACK AND WHITE
NEGATIVES, DYES, AND COMPUTER GRAPHICS

183

April Rapier

PORTRAIT OF ARTIST ALAIN CLEMENT,
FOR A PROJECT DOCUMENTING
ARTISTS IN TEXAS

184

John Labbé

HOLLYWOOD BEACH IN FLORIDA
ON THANKSGIVING DAY, 1989,
PHOTO TAKEN WITH A PINHOLE CAMERA

185

E l a i n e   F i s h e r

THIS SELF ASSIGNED PIECE COMBINES
COMPUTER GRAPHICS WITH A PHOTO IMAGE.

William Rivelli

FIVE PHOTOGRAPHS FROM A SELF-ASSIGNED
ARCHITECTURE SERIES

RINELLI'S MAUSOLEUM

(Opposite)

SOLID COLUMNS

188

STAIRWAY TO ABOVE

189

SPEARHEADS AND SNOW BUSHES

190
(Opposite)

ARCHWAY TO NOWHERE

Index

PHOTOGRAPHERS

Abbas
c/o Magnum
20 Rue Des Grand Augustins
Paris, France 75006
Plates 33-34

Max Aguilera-Hellweg
1316 ½ Westerly Terrace
Los Angeles, CA 90026
Plates 24-26

Josef Astor
154 W. 57th St.
New York, NY 10019
Plates 67, 73-75

Richard Avedon
407 E. 75 St.
New York, NY 10021
Plate 32

Bruno Barbey
c/o Magnum
20 Rue Des Grand Augustins
Paris, France 75006
Plate 127

Christopher Boas
20 Bond St.
New York, NY 10012
Plates 155-156

Daniel Borris
126 11th St. S.E.
Washington, D.C. 20003
Plate 157

The Douglas Brothers
c/o ONYX
7515 Beverly Blvd.
Los Angeles, CA 90036
Plate 4

Paul Chesley
1280 Ute Ave.
Aspen, CO 81611
Plate 130

Tony Costa
1321 N. Genesee
Los Angeles, CA 90046
Plate 55

Lee Crum
1536 Terpsichore St.
New Orleans, LA 70130
Plate 95-97

Craig Cutler
39 Walker St.
New York, NY 10013
Plate 154

Skip Dean
9 Davies Ave., Ste. 200
Toronto, ONT. M4M 2A6
Canada
Plate 170-171

Jay Dickman
5650 Blue Sage Dr.
Littleton, CO 80123
Plate 128

Phillip Dixon
c/o Allen Hardy
1680 North Vine
Suite 112
Los Angeles, CA 90028
Plate 69

John Dyer
107 Blue Star
San Antonio, TX 78204
Plates 158-160

Herman LeRoy Emmet
18 Elm Street
Southampton, NY 11968
Plates 131-135

Elaine Fisher
7 McTernan St.
Cambridge, MA 02139
Plate 185

Timothy Greenfield-Sanders
c/o Stockland/Martell
5 Union Sq. West
New York, NY 10003
Plates 111-113

Guzman
31 W. 31st St.
New York, NY 10001
Plate 61

Mick Hales
c/o Helen Pratt
271 Madison Ave
New York, NY 10016
Plate 76

Mark Hanauer
1153 N. Las Palmas
Hollywood, CA 90038
Plate 181

C.B. Harding
660 N. Thompson
Portland, OR 97227
Plate 118

Marc Hauser
1810 W. Cortland
Chicago, IL 60622
Plates 114-116

Gregory Heisler
568 Broadway
New York, NY 10012
Plate 117

Timothy Hursley
1911 West Markham
Little Rock, AR 72205
Plates 121-125

Gabriella Imperatori
438 Broome St.
New York, NY 10013
Plates 43-47, 142-143

Silas Jackson
368 Broadway
New York, NY 10013
Plate 175

Nick Kelsh
211 North 13th St.
Philadelphia, PA 19107
Plate 126

Geof Kern
1337 Crampton
Dallas, TX 75207
Plates 6, 7, 8-11, 36, 77, 120, 136, 137

Nick Knight
16 Arlington Rd.
Petersham, Richmond
Surrey, U.K.
Plate 71

John Labbé
97 3rd Ave.
New York, NY 10003
Plate 184

Annie Leibovitz
c/o Art & Commerce
108 W. 18th St.
New York, NY 10011
Plates 12-14, 15, 22-26

Christopher Little
4 W. 22nd St.
New York, NY 10010
Plate 41

Mark Mainguy
c/o Greg Le Froy and Associates
197 A Eastern Ave.
Toronto, ONT M5A 1H9
Canada
Plate 68

Mary Ellen Mark
134 Spring St.
New York, NY 10012
Plates 37-39

Kurt Markus
237 ¹/₂ Main St.
Kalispell, MT 59901
Plates 84-94, 145-150

Dilip Mehta
c/o Contact Press Images
116 East 27th St.
New York, NY 10016
Plate 129

Sheila Metzner
310 Riverside Dr., Ste. 200
New York, NY 10025
Plates 63, 172-173, 176

Eleni Mylonas
148 Greene St.
New York, NY 10012
Plates 161-162

Charlie Pizzarello
15 W. 18th St.
New York, NY 10011
Plate 180

Lisa Powers
12 E. 86th St.
New York, NY 10028
Plate 48, 49

Daniel Proctor
170 W. 25th St., #2C
New York, NY 10001
Plate 167

April Rapier
6340 Mercer St.
Houston, TX 77005
Plate 183

Michael Regnier
905 Broadway, 4th Fl.
Kansas City, MO 64105
Plates 98-99

Jon A. Rembold
15823 Easthaven Ct.
Bowie, MD 20716
Plate 168

William Rivelli
303 Park Ave. South
New York, NY 10010
Plates 186-190

Herb Ritts
7927 Hillside Ave.
Los Angeles, CA 90046
Plates 5, 62, 64, 65

Deborah Samuel
104 Sumach St.
Toronto, ONT. M5A 3J9
Canada
Plate 78

Chris Sanders
130 W. 23rd St.
New York, NY 10011
Plate 72

Rocky Schenck
2210 North Beachwood Dr.
Los Angeles, CA 90068
Plates 50-54

Mark Seliger
251 West 19th St.
New York, NY 10011
Plate 42

Jeremy Shatan
379 Parkside Ave.
Brooklyn, NY 11226
Plate 83

Charles Shotwell
2111 N. Clifton
Chicago, IL 60614
Plate 40

Chip Simons
26 W. 27th St.
New York, NY 10001
Plates 101-110

Jim Sims
c/o Cobb & Friend
3232 McKinney, #1260
Dallas, TX 75204
Plates 144, 163-164

Neal Slavin
c/o Barbara Von Schreiber
315 Central Park West
New York, NY 10025
Plates 79-82

Brian Smale
c/o Sharpshooter Studios
387 Richmond St. East
Toronto, ONT. M5A 1P6
Canada
Plates 28-31, 70, 138

George Steinmetz
662 Waller St.
San Francisco, CA 94117
Plate 169

Sandra Tasca
P.O. Box 80253
San Marino, CA 91118
Plate 182

Walter Urie
2204 N. Ross St.
Santa Ana, CA 92706
Plates 140-141

Nick Vedros
6411 Wyandotte
Kansas City, MO 64113
Plate 119

William Volckening
673 Mill St.
Moorestown, NJ 08057
Plate 151

Albert Watson
797 Washington St.
New York, NY 10014
Plates 1-3, 16-21, 56-60

Stuart Watson
620 Moulton Ave.
Los Angeles, CA 90031
Plate 66

Daniel Winters
46 Laight, #3R
New York, NY 10013
Plates 152-153

James Wojcik
265 Mott St., #4
New York, NY 10012
Plates 177-179

Timothy White
448 W. 37th St.
Studio 7C
New York, NY 10018
Plates 23, 139

Robert Whitman
1181 Broadway, 7th Fl.
New York, NY 10001
Plate 35

Ethel Wolvovitz
305 Ocean Pkwy.
Brooklyn, NY 11218
Plates 165-166

Taro Yamasaki
638 Bloomer Rd.
Rochester, MI 48063
Plate 100